Hares

Ashley Lee

Explore other books at:
WWW.ENGAGEBOOKS.COM

VANCOUVER, B.C.

 WWW.ENGAGEBOOKS.COM

Hares: Level 3
Animals That Make a Difference!
Lee, Ashley, 1995
Text © 2024 Engage Books
Design © 2024 Engage Books

Edited by: A.R. Roumanis and Melody Sun
Design by: Mandy Christiansen

Text set in Arial Regular.
Chapter headings set in Nathaniel-19.

FIRST EDITION / FIRST PRINTING

All rights reserved. No part of this book may be stored in a retrieval system, reproduced or transmitted in any form or by any other means without written permission from the publisher or a licence from the Canadian Copyright Licensing Agency. Critics and reviewers may quote brief passages in connection with a review or critical article in any media.

Every reasonable effort has been made to contact the copyright holders of all material reproduced in this book.

LIBRARY AND ARCHIVES CANADA CATALOGUING IN PUBLICATION

Title: Hares / Ashley Lee.
Names: Lee, Ashley, author.
Description: Series statement: Animals that make a difference

Identifiers: Canadiana (print) 20230448542 | Canadiana (ebook) 20230448569
ISBN 978-1-77878-621-1 (hardcover)
ISBN 978-1-77878-622-8 (softcover)
ISBN 978-1-77878-623-5 (epub)
ISBN 978-1-77878-624-2 (pdf)

Subjects:
LCSH: Hares—Juvenile literature.
LCSH: Human-animal relationships—Juvenile literature.

Classification: LCC QL737.P94 C38 2023 | DDC J599.885—DC23

This project has been made possible in part by the Government of Canada.

Contents

- 4   What Are Hares?
- 6   A Closer Look
- 8   Where Do Hares Live?
- 10   What Do Hares Eat?
- 12   How Do Hares Talk to Each Other?
- 14   Hare Life Cycle
- 16   Curious Facts About Hares
- 18   Kinds of Hares
- 20   How Hares Help Earth
- 22   How Hares Help Other Animals
- 24   How Hares Help Humans
- 26   Hares in Danger
- 28   How to Help Hares
- 30   Quiz

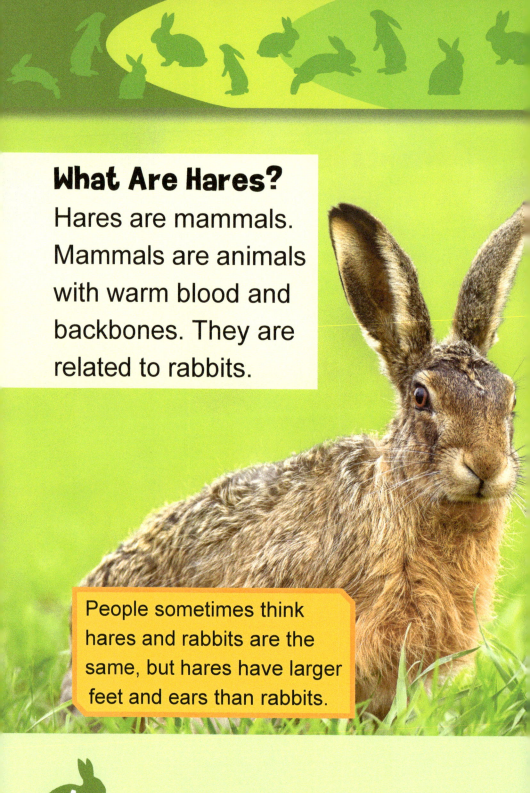

What Are Hares?

Hares are mammals. Mammals are animals with warm blood and backbones. They are related to rabbits.

People sometimes think hares and rabbits are the same, but hares have larger feet and ears than rabbits.

Hares are nocturnal. This means they are active at night. This helps them stay away from **predators** who are active during the day. Foxes, coyotes, and bears all like to eat hares.

KEY WORD

Predators: animals that eat other animals.

A Closer Look

Hares are usually a gray-brown color. Some hares that live in the north are white or turn white when the weather gets really cold. They are about 16 to 28 inches (40 to 70 centimeters) long.

A hare's feet can be up to 5.9 inches (15 cm) long! They help them jump long distances.

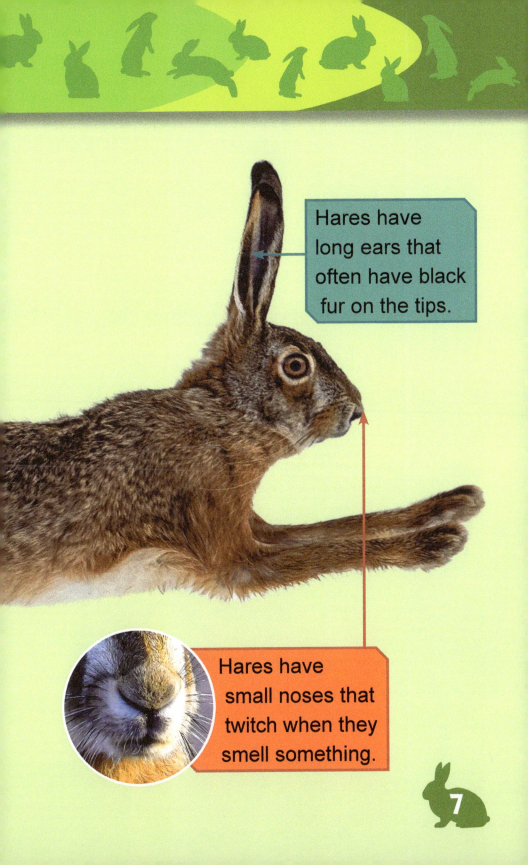

Hares have long ears that often have black fur on the tips.

Hares have small noses that twitch when they smell something.

Where Do Hares Live?

Hares live in many different **habitats**. Some like cold snowy areas. Others like hot deserts. Most hares like to live in open fields.

KEY WORD

Habitats: natural places where plants and animals live.

Hares live all over the world. Abyssinian hares live in East Africa. Alaskan hares mostly live in Alaska in the United States. Korean hares are found in Korea and China.

What Do Hares Eat?

Hares are herbivores. This means they only eat plants. They eat lots of leaves, grass, and tree bark.

Hares will sometimes eat their own poop. They do this because plants can be hard for them to **digest**. Plants that have been turned into poop are easier for hares to digest.

KEY WORD

Digest: the act of eating food and breaking it down so the body can turn it into energy.

Some hares can eat up to 2.2 pounds (1 kilogram) of food every day.

How Do Hares Talk to Each Other?

Hares mostly talk to each other by thumping their back feet against the ground. Sometimes they will snort when upset. Males will sometimes make a clicking noise to get females to come close to them.

Male hares will chase female hares when they want to have babies with them. If the female does not want to have babies with the male, she may stand on her back legs and **box** with him. This will sometimes go on for weeks.

KEY WORD

Box: fight using fists.

Hare Life Cycle

Most female hares give birth to between three and six babies at one time. Some hares can give birth three or four times in a single year. This means a hare could have 24 babies in one year!

Baby hares are called leverets. They are born covered in hair and with their eyes open. Their mothers leave them alone for most of the day. They only come back to feed their babies.

Baby hares are able to run a few minutes after birth. They can live without their mothers at just a few weeks old. They can start to have their own babies when they are about eight months old.

Hares spend most of their lives alone. Many hares only go near other hares when they want to make babies. Most hares only live for three to four years.

Curious Facts About Hares

Hares grow new fur two times every year.

Some hares can run 43.5 miles (70 kilometers) per hour.

Hares are able to sit very still and blend in with their surroundings so they are not seen by predators.

A hare's front teeth never stop growing. Chewing plants helps stop them from getting too long.

Baby hares have no smell. This helps them hide from predators.

Hares often run in a zigzag pattern when being chased by other animals.

Kinds of Hares

There are about 30 different kinds of hares. One of the most common kinds is the European hare. They are also called brown hares.

Mountain hares are one of the hares that change color when it gets cold. Their ears are shorter than the European hare's.

Despite their name, black-tailed jackrabbits are actually hares. They are often found in the fields of farms.

The Indian hare is also called the black-naped hare. They have a patch of black fur on the back of their neck.

How Hares Help Earth

Many hares eat seeds when they eat plants. The seeds stay in their bodies as they move to different areas. These seeds then come out in their poop.

This allows plants to spread to new areas. These seeds would not be able to move to new areas on their own. Hare poop also helps the seeds grow into healthy plants.

This process is called seed dispersal.

How Hares Help Other Animals

Snowshoe hares and lynx in Canada and Alaska have a special relationship. The number of lynx depends on the number of snowshoe hares. When there are lots of snowshoe hares, lynx have lots of food. Lynx have more babies when they have lots of food.

More lynx means more hares get eaten. As the number of snowshoe hares goes down, lynx have less food. This means their numbers go down as well. Fewer lynx gives snowshoe hares time to have more babies. This then gives lynx lots of food again.

How Hares Help Humans

Many early **Indigenous** communities hunted hares for food. They would also use hare fur to make clothing. This helped them stay warm. Some communities still hunt hares for food.

KEY WORD

Indigenous: the first people to live in a place.

Scientists are studying **stress** in hares. They are trying to find out if a mother can pass stress on to her babies. They hope this will help them understand stress in humans.

KEY WORD

Stress: when a living thing feels uncomfortable about something that is happening.

Hares in Danger

Some kinds of hares are endangered. This means there are very few of them left. Many hares lose their homes when people build bigger farms and cities.

Hainan hares and Tehuantepec (tuh-waan-tah-pec) jackrabbits are both endangered.

Many farmers use chemicals called herbicides on the plants they grow. Herbicides kill any weeds in the area. These chemicals can also kill the wild plants that hares eat. This leaves hares with very little food.

How to Help Hares

If you find a baby hare, leave it where you found it. It may look **abandoned**, but its mother is coming back for it. Mother hares are often only near their babies late at night and early in the morning.

Plant a wildlife-friendly garden. Use plants that hares can eat and hide in. Do not use harmful chemicals like herbicides on your plants.

KEY WORD

Abandoned: left alone without any help.

Quiz

Test your knowledge of hares by answering the following questions. The questions are based on what you have read in this book. The answers are listed on the bottom of the next page.

1. What are hares related to?

2. Where do most hares like to live?

3. What will hares sometimes do when upset?

4. What are baby hares called?

5. What are scientists studying in hares?

6. What should you do if you find a baby hare?

Explore other books in the Animals That Make a Difference series

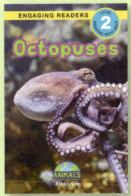

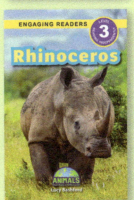

Visit www.engagebooks.com to explore more Engaging Readers.

Answers: 1. Rabbits 2. In open fields 3. Snort 4. Leverets 5. Stress 6. Leave it where you found it

Milton Keynes UK
Ingram Content Group UK Ltd.
UKHW051658081024
449373UK00018B/272